Choosing Charlie

By Cheryl Ann Whitsett

Acknowledgements

Thank you Thomas Whitsett for being my biggest fan. Your undying love for me is what makes me continue to do what I do. For that I will always be grateful.

I am Charlie and I am almost three years old. My mommy and daddy were looking for another black cat like my sister Sia. Black cats are that hardest to adopt because of peoples fear of them. They have always been associated with witches in past centuries and it has lived on even today. Sia is my girl but I have a story to tell about how my mommy and daddy made my life wonderful.

Every spring is kitten season here in Jacksonville Florida and the shelters are over run by kittens because people will not spay or neuter their pets. Mommy and daddy were in Pet Smart one day looking for another black cat and mommy saw a couple but as my daddy walked past me, I reached out my paw and touched him on his arm.

He saw his furry little son and told mommy I was the one he wanted because he picked us. When I heard daddy say that I was so excited that I was finally going to go to my forever home.

I was packaged in a cardboard box and tried my best all the way home to get out of that box. They told mommy and daddy I was only six months old but when I went to the vet she told mommy I was a year old. Mommy said I was too big to be only six months old.

Two days after I was home I came down sick with an upper respiratory infection from the kennel. Mommy was very scared because I wasn't breathing too well and she took me to the pet emergency room. Not only was I sick but in a few days the other two cats would be sick also. Buffy is my other sister and she is old as dirt. Mommy was very mad at Pet Smart for adopting me out sick.

It was a sneezing, coughing so you can't rest kind of mess at my new house and mommy was tired. She gave us medicine around the clock and after two or three weeks we finally were all clear of the nonsense.

Once I was well, I started playing with my big sister dog Tinkerbelle. The other cats hated me for a while so she was the only one I could play with. It was worse than an opossum hissing at a human. Seriously these cats had it out for me for making them sick. Mommy knew I was feeling better when I started stalking the girls. Sia and Buffy hated me. Baxter is an old fat cat so I didn't mess with him. He is the only one that had claws. The girls didn't so I chased them. I was going to make them like me no matter what. Well that was a nice thought but even after living here with them for almost three years now, they don't find this handsome fur man very funny.

Whenever mommy changes the bed, I think it's a game and I get up on the bed and hide under the covers. She covers me all up and then takes pictures of me as a lump in the bed. I hear her telling me to stop it but I think it is really a fun game to play.

Mommy doesn't really know how I ended up at the shelter but she can assume I was a brat and my other parents didn't want me. I am a food beggar and a play maker so mommy and daddy think I was raised with dogs.

My parents make some tasty food and I don't know why the other three cats are so stupid not to beg for food. They just eat their cat food like good little kitties and the dogs and I sit at the table and beg for food. Mommy has a double glass table so I get in between the table glass and look upside down at them until they give me food. It's fun and I will touch my daddy so he knows I am there to give me food.

Every morning I sit and look out the windows and watch the squirrels running up and down the fence. I start to chatter hoping they will come in the house so I can chase them.

I have it so rough here. I get so much attention because I am ornery and chase the girls and the dogs and even try to play with mommy but she doesn't appreciate me letting her pet me then I bite her and run. She doesn't think it is as funny as I do. Well I have to admit, biting the hand that feeds you is not a cool thing to do. She also refuses to give me table food so I resort to daddy. When he goes away for work, he is gone sometimes forever and I don't get anything while he is gone except cat food. I am not a cat I am a furry person with feelings and I protest and do bad things like knock all of mommy's nick knack's down off of the end tables.

I chase Sia and mommy gets mad because I pull her hair out and mommy has enough hair to clean up every day. She is OCD about cleaning the floors I think.

If Sia would just let me be her guy, I would be a happy fur man. Mommy says she will never be my girl because I am too rough and make her yell. Tinkerbelle my dog sister is the only one I can play rough with because she doesn't have a shut off button and she wants to play every day all day and mommy doesn't always get to sleep through the night because Tinkerbelle has to go outside to play in the dark. Even I sleep all night with mommy. Sometimes I think mommy would really like to have her bed but we all sleep with her. When daddy comes home mommy sometimes sleeps at the bottom of the bed because we are all crammed up at the top and we don't move.

I have to admit that mommy buys some darn nice quilts for the bed and it feels good to lay on but then she complains about the hair. I think she would really love to shave us all bald but we would look too funny. Mommy has this super-duper machine that vacuums and cleans the floors. She loves it. Well who wouldn't when there are so many of us. Mommy and daddy love to rescue animals and I was a lucky boy to be picked.

Mommy heard a bunch of commotion going on in the bathroom. She got scared but she always looks anyway. I found amusement behind the shower curtain because it makes an awesome noise when you try to climb it. That fun didn't last long because mommy was not happy about holes in her shower curtain.

I love boxes and bags and we always have plenty because I heard my daddy say something about all the things that mommy buys. It's true though. We get packages every single day. I didn't know it was stuff mommy was buying. She has this site call eBay and I think she would like to list all of us on the days we are all bad.

I like to be outside but sometimes I escape and don't come home for a day or two. Mommy cries so loud I can hear her blocks away. I just want to chase bugs and lizards but mommy is afraid I will get hit by a car or something. She doesn't know that I already survived that nonsense before I came to the shelter. I think it's fun when mommy or daddy leave to go to work and I slip out the door and run like heck under the cars. They have to try to find a way to get me back inside so mommy and daddy turn these things on that are called cars and it scares me so I run back to the door to be let in. Mommy said I was going to catch these things called fleas and bring them in the house to the other cats. I don't know what a flea is but a bird would be much nicer.

So let me tell you about all my siblings. Buffy is a 15 year old calico kitty and she does not like to play. She sits her butt in a throne like chair and looks at us with disgust. She is the old queen that thinks she rules the roost, however I am the leader of the cat pack.

Baxter is a blonde maincoon kitty who is big and fat. He reminds me of Garfield. Every morning he begs mommy for treats but I am glad he does. We all get treats every morning. But big boy eats everyone else's if he gets done with his first.

Sia, my girl, is a black kitty. She is the sweetest of all the kitties but I chase her and try to make her love me, but she screams and then mommy gets mad at me because her hair goes flying everywhere.

You see how handsome I am. Mommy and daddy say I am the most handsome boy on the earth but I hear her tell all the animals that. I have never seen myself in a mirror but I sure feel handsome and playful.

I stalk all the humans in this house and either bite them and run or paw them and run. Mommy says something like I am getting declawed but I will have to think hard about that one. Who will help me if I get out? Oh that's right I am not supposed to be outside. I don't understand all the hype about me being outside. It's spring time and lots of lizards are just waiting for me. Mommy should be happy that we keep the bugs and lizards at bay for her. She doesn't like spiders or roaches and we get them every time. I even carry them to her bed so she can see they won't hurt her ever again. She screams in fear and I laugh to myself. We have a small petting zoo and she is scared of a little bug. Who knew?

Mommy caught me sitting on the kitchen table. I was stalking the dogs. They can't reach me up here so it is kind of funny to me but mommy was mad. I always get cat hair on everything she owns. You would think one day she would quit cleaning and relax like we do. I think she is an ocd cleaning lady. I don't think she goes to that place called work. She gets up, gets dressed and leaves because we aggravate her to no end. She still says she loves us even when we are bad. But I have to admit I am the troublesome cat. I can't help it. These other three cats are useless in the cat world. I get all the bugs and lizards and my reward is table food.

This is my dog brother Jake. He is a fat stack. He is almost a hundred pounds but he is very gentle playing with me. He doesn't know what to think about my claws going in his nose. My other dog sister Tinkerbelle is a hot mess. She does not play nice. She puts my whole head in her mouth but not to hurt me. She is playing and would never hurt me like that. It goes to show that dogs can be gentle with cats but not with each other. It makes no sense to me that she loves Jake and us and wants to rip off mommy's grand dogs' face. Her grand dog is named Sasha and she is a chow. Her and my sister dog Tinkerbelle hate each other and have to be kept separated all the time. Sasha loves to chase me too. I always aggravate them because they can't catch me. I am fast like a squirrel hopping on a fence.

The dogs are always chasing squirrels but they cannot catch them. I sit at the door and laugh at them. I really think I talk bad about them, but they act like they don't care what I say.

This is Sasha the grand dog and she is cute as anything. She loves all of us cats but another girl dog is out of the question. They could play so good together if Sasha just wouldn't growl at Tinkerbelle. I say let them duke it out but mommy says no. She wouldn't want any of them to get hurt.

Words from my mommy:

Each year 8 million dogs and cats are euthanized that are healthy and could make nice pets. People need to learn to spay or neuter your animals to prevent more and more euthanasia.   No animal should die this way because they are thrown away like garbage. If anyone could see how they complete this process it is very horrible what they go through.

Charlie was a fortunate cat to get a good home with parents that love him. He is funny but sometimes a little mischievous.   If I could save them all I would.

I am proud to live in a city where we have a no kill status. Every three months we have a big adoption event. 1,000 animals are saved but within a few weeks the shelters are full again. Animals deserve to be loved and treated with kindness. We domesticated them. We wanted them for pets but refused to fix them so now they are over populated. If you have feral cats call your local shelter. They will spay or neuter them and release them back in your neighborhood. It's still a life even if they are wild.

We as humans can be a voice for these animals. They need love just like humans. You wouldn't drop your baby off at a shelter to be euthanized so why would you do it for your own pet.

I am Charlie and I am love!

I am Jake and I am love!

I am Sasha and I am love!

I am Tinkerbelle and I am love!

I am Binky and I am love.

My babies forever. I am their mommy and I love them!

About the Author

Cheryl Whitsett is an animal activist trying to make a difference to animal's lives. She has four rescue cats, two rescue dogs, two rescue iguanas and two rescue snakes. All of these books are about her animals and her undying love to make sure they have a good life.

Other Books Published By This Author

Dream to Awaken From One Click of Death

A Dream of Death Forgotten the Sequel

The Prevalence of Love

Saving Tinkerbelle

How I met my Best Friend

How a Dinosaur Became a Princess

Choosing Charlie

Debts of Life a Divine Book of Poetry

True Cupid

www.ingramcontent.com/pod-product-compliance
Lightning Source LLC
Chambersburg PA
CBHW060825290526
45792CB00005BB/1808